ERIC REYMOND
NIMRODIA

new texture

A New Texture book

Text copyright © 2004, 2007, 2008, 2011, 2018 by Eric Reymond

Cover art by Oliver Reymond

Designed and edited by Wyatt Doyle

NewTexture.com

Booksellers: *Nimrodia* and other New Texture books
are available through Ingram Book Company

ISBN 978-1-943444-91-5

First New Texture softcover edition: March 2018
Printed in the United States

10 9 8 7 6 5 4 3 2 1

For R, L, O

Contents

Part 1

Tur-Tur

1.

Stare at the tower in Bruegel. Consider his design. The faces that the façade's middle arches make, their windows and open mouths that communicate

no expression, but stare and stare into the Netherlandish flats. One can hardly come to the painting with a knowledge of illustrations for children's books and not think such detailing cheeky. "The impact of this adventure." You think

2.

The work proceeds, the mason says to the grass. Which all his underlings affirm

The king speaks to the masons to hear his counselors listening:
        We engage endless progress
                    — to move the earth

3.

The polyspastos pulls. It is spring, according to the painter. The workers laugh, file, and hammer. The tower promises survival from any future, stepping alive into heaven,

feeling one's face against God's . . .

4.

Stare inside the red marble

                       arcades. Vaticans

      of spirit. Red like the organs

          of an animal, but marble-cold

          The way forward

     "We are the lever,"

          the king famously says

5.

Turn leisurely

        the painting speaks

             to our disaster

We are ants in an idea. We are instruments for its inception. And ruin.
As one we work

         We turn out space from air. We speak as
one. Even uncertain what it means

6.

The scaffoldings branch and wye beneath the arches' browing
   The foot is broken though the head is being polished

"Beginning is what makes the whole's first half
   so beginning, he made the world"

so runs one of Nimrod's sonnets

7.

The masons have brought their lunch and their mallets. They lay their chisels on the stone
They hear the king and they do not

     Les voussoirs sont . . . the masons
      in their evening's slumber
         beneath the vault
     of sky

8.

The tower must be made of circles moving outwardly inwardly, the king once advised, it must be an eye

> The corkscrewing
> edge pulls in sky,
>> in blue, in breath, in

9.

You walk into the interior halls and feel the air beneath your feet. The floors are wooden, with small holes drilled every other inch; beneath the floor, wind pushes from outside, through vents, up around your ankles, up your shins, through the folds of your cowl or veil. This is the sense you get. This is the design. Of lifting. Of feeling air

10.

In the buttress sheds, the workers repeat the rumor that the tower, when finished, will be built of 72 materials

(including lime, cement, earth, pitch, blood, and clay), corresponding to the 72 counselors, 72 artificers, 72 masons

to the width of the path circling up its side: 72 paces in width to each layer 72 cubits in height, nearer heaven

The masons remark on the flight of birds. "What do you call a group of geese?" one asks another

11.

In the arcades, one engineer ascends in his frock. How many steps, he says to himself, how many steps

                    Is it a question or an answer? There are as many
                    steps

The distance between heaven and heaven is 500 years. Beneath the groin vaults, stop and ask nothing but to repeat

12.

We have made this world, the engineers like to say, from our own conceptions. We have drawn from our own minds all the materials employed

>The tower is made of only nine:
>>noun, pronoun, verb,
>>>adverb, participle, con-
>junction, pre-
>>>position, and inter-
>>>jection.

Words are strong as baked bricks.

13.

And you catch yourself thinking

>Our present plan
>>leads up
>to open
>>an entirely different
>>>course
>>to the understanding,

and one unattempted
>>and unknown . . .

14.

The king turns to his counselors,

          To know something is to find a place one is at home. To know something is to make a world. To know something is to discover one paradise.

          Without shadows or evening

with alternate liquids and solids.

15.

The tower listens like an open ear. Half-finished, it repeats its chambers and tunnels. Like a labyrinth's. Its hissing secret, like the sound of a lung expanding and contracting.

16.

Walk the corridors

        and it is like walking

                between stiff gills of a giant

    fish. You are someplace

      you have never been.

17.

    Each person is a tower.

Is this the tower's thought or is it ours?

Walk, one chamber at a time. Listening to the blood of the ear: shack,
pear, son . . .

18.

Why is its shape the shape of purgatory? What was Bruegel's idea?

What is the mountain that hides beneath the tower? What is its name? How could such rock sneak into the tower? It says that the tower is not all design.

The lateen mizzens fill and slack, fill and slack.

The world, seen from heaven, is another carrack scything blue.

19.

One scribe tells another: There is an account in our records of a lazy son of a prince, who once sought to find transcendence by eating bookworms that had passed through the holy word itself.

20.

Knowledge is breath. But what does it mean between tyranny and oblivion?

> That knowledge hath in it
>> somewhat of the serpent
> is also well known.
> No one can predict with
>> certainty
>>> what the ultimate meaning

will be.

21.

Who will be the first to climb through the window of sun? the workers ask themselves at lunch.

Their supervisors respond:

> It will not be one
> person making this daring climb,
>> it will be an entire
> race, for all of us must
>> work to   put him there.

Do they believe?

22.

Imagination must not be stopped, Nimrod thought, or, Imagination
cannot meet an end.

So, he is said to have said "Raphel may amecche zabi almi."

23.

Culex, the king began to think of the Vergilian poem, swatting and
swatting. Like the memory of something

> A nursling of humid air,
> > the king hears in his sleep

> Is thy life more precious than mine own?
> > Shunned destruction doth destruction render

Sometimes the smallest thing hunts you
> > down

24.

Take the tower in the palm.

            What is the answer to the sky's question?
        Is the dark finger of cloud pointing down?

The heavens are purple and water green
Where would someone fall out of the sky? Fall in?

25.

The worker's mess is thatched and warm. It is low. It is fragile. It is built
to be taken down.

26.
The tower sits like a buddha.

Knowing is only half way

           The universe is multi-tiered
           From the atom down

27.
For what is

           ambition, but the inner question

    that never ceases asking.

28.

The point of a spear, held up to the sky?
     No, this is not, the king thinks,

      a battle between two things.
  It is their melding.

    One thing from the next.
  Nothing is itself alone,

    nor are the heavens.

29.

Stare at the painting. Someone else is eating or opening a window or just walking along, painting a thing that cannot be a painting.

Part 2

The Similitudes of Nimrod

0.

Creation is a stomach within a stomach within a stomach.

1.

All knowledge and wonder is the impression of pleasure in itself.

2.

A tower can be made with only two bricks or two words.

3.

The inverse of a tower is brutality.

4.

The universe is

a circle,   the earth

a point,   the heavens

archers,   accidents

arrows   and a person

a target never escaped.

5.

Words are daughters of earth and things the sons of heaven. Giants roam earth building meaning.

6.

The tower must be made of rings moving outwardly, ceaselessly.

7.

The truth of being and the truth of knowing are one, differing no more than the direct beam and the beam reflected.

8.

It would be madness to suppose that things which have never been performed can be performed without employing something hitherto untried.

9.

Inside, the tower is not an edifice, but rather something like a burrow that must be continually dug and that is never finished.

10.

Heaven will open to us; and our eagerness to share its meaning should not be governed by the efforts or impediments of others.

11.

There is a ghost inside the heart that says you have been invented for this very purpose, that says the earth is a globe, the spheres can be surmounted, and the angels are trumpets in the wind.

12.

Our only remaining hope and salvation is to begin the whole labor of the mind again; not leaving it to itself, but directing it perpetually from the very first, and attaining our end as it were by mechanical aid.

Part 3

Cloud Study

Repeat above

the icon shiftingly

scumble bumble

model life:

the untrunked tree

the looking glass verb

the argument around sight

Filled Like a Brush

       with inner cadmium,
I don't need to vandalize
empty hours with exercise,
or stir my eyes into coffee cups
rationalizing what needs reading,
what letters turn pleonastic,
which diphthongs monophthongize,

I let myself mix with the medium of
façade, with windows like a Dutch master
who paints what is transparent.

Or, like a Rauschenberg who erased
his DeKooning, frenzied strokes
vanishing beneath frenzied strokes:
plump breasts and wild eyes,
the pleading yellow-green of desire,
giving way to lawnmower blades,
unmade beds, and a cat consuming Judas.

Aerialists

The uterine sun.

Awake in the redness.

Tears like sweet beer.

You only begin
to feel your weight
falling eighteen times
the speed of peals.

You become meteoric,
sterling slicing
through layered spheres
(exo, iono, thermo) —
an ancient signal
mortals had passed
into the driver's seat,
into gods.

Dissolving incandescent
into what is not quite
solid, liquid, or gas.

The Poet in Miniature

Rapture forbids depicting anything
                              real.

The whole garden is
                    just thirty centimeters
in width.

An eye pops open one millimeter
above his mouth.
                    A moustache whisps
imperfects.
                              The ladies train
white gardenias —
                    Chinese clouds
churn over Persia.

No one reveals consternation
at arms that throw
                    no shadows,
but rich, satin hues.

A third foot slinks out of his robe.
                              The ladies
weave their extra hands through stoles.

Mouths invisible
                    behind kerchiefs.

Cursive fruit hang all about,
                    no ornament
of words,
                    feeling more than food.

How to Be a Swan

Begin by folding yourself in half, along a diagonal line. Breathe. You may unfold yourself

Remember that this is only one beginning for beauty, poise, and serenity

When you turn your corners inward, imagine your hands on your hips and pulling your elbows into your stomach

recount, simultaneously, that on the night of November 18, 2012, someone was stabbed in the neck

in the Westin Hotel in downtown Chicago, during a failed robbery, while you sat in your hotel room

Fold your arms around again, you should feel yourself narrowing into a point, a needle of concentration

Recount also that on that same night, thieves made off with hundreds of dollars of apparel

from a downtown Chicago store, after being fired upon by a cop

Fold yourself in half at the waist, so your feet meet your face, then, turn your feet downward at the ankle

Relax your legs ever so slightly. Your feet a head. Your legs a neck and your head a tail

The pain is extraordinary, the value unclear

Part 4

On the Making of Words

1.
Life ends, but a serious work of scholarship
expands
            like air.

Knowledge should know no end.

To stop learning, as they say,
                is to corner a unicorn.

2.
The emperor believed himself beyond the trivial. In the sixth century
he wrote his golden work.

Of the unknown number of books it is said to have contained, only 14
survive in fragments, among which are: *The Manner
of Collecting Books*, *The Writing of Books*, and *On the Making
of Words*.

3.
But, he is remembered best for what is lost.

The historian records how he walked into the Hall of Bamboos and
ordered that all the books, some 140,000, be burned.

Only then did he decide
                he must also die.

Stopped, he declared: "Civilizations end."

4.

And afterward he worked on his masterpiece,
    but allowed no one to read it.

It grew and grew.

When he would return from the provinces, others would plead with him to have just a glance.

But, he never let two eyes fall on it.

5.

He was left with only one eye. Disease took the other when he was young.

So, it is said, his wife would only make up half her face.

And he cried only a single line.

6.

At the end, he sat alone for years
    memorizing who was born to whom.

Great strings the generations became,
    father wove into son
        into grandson and grandson.

Until he felt himself become like one of those blown eggs

    that hang each spring
    in the windows

not knowing
    whether he contained an emptiness

or was a buttress against the infinite

                         expanding all around

     him.

The Stylite

Honing patience into patience, unsheltering each thought in sky.

One link in a chain of quiet, the ascetic sat on his pillar.

Some thought him a fable, as Theodoret's pilgrim asked him directly once: "Are you human or angel?"

Never turning his face from the west, never sitting down, remaining ten years in a tub suspended in air.

He slept only one hour a night, never lying down.

35 years in the space of a tabletop.

Before he thought up pillar-sitting, he had made a cell of a dry cistern between mountain paths, where he slept unnoticed, a dry, black wick.

Until those seeking blessings found him and sat on the cell's lip like sparrows waiting to be fed. They cannot be stopped, he had thought.

I must ascend.

The fire came every night, transformed all that wind couldn't waste.

Fronds lined his small black mantle and stabbed like teeth.

His stomach churned and bled on a hunger he kept to himself.

Some said it was "ambrosial." He would not say this. His thirst was never clear. Everything burned in stillness to be

heard and felt. The pillar, the desert, the heart.

What was between heaven and earth
                            where Hera once rode her
        chariot to Troy?

Where else? he asked. If not . . . He pondered all that prayers left.

A speckless vastness. Solitude at work. Where each sureness meets the question of air.

The Legend of the First Emperor

The year I was emperor fire was discovered
                              earth grew

waters ballooned waves
                    air was stacked high over every tree, higher
                    than even before, equal in every direction —

and beauty was measured in breadth and width,
                    innate, as it was, in every limb.

The year I was emperor I declared nothing further would come
into being
                    and nothing would pass away.

And then I rescinded.

My mathematicians nodded: "Here, there's no why."

"I know how it will end," I said one day
                    when my mouth was a sword.

I will write my classic during a single night
                    and vanish into the west:

So full of joy
          I will be changed entirely.

Eratosthenes

He realized he did not know whether
he was
        listening to the pens lift
and fall across the tables
                or to doves pecking
the hearts out of worms on the sill.

His job might be done.
        And he turned restlessly inside
his gummy words.

Knowledge must be stored, he thought,
and this is a very Alexandrian thought.

But tested in the light of the day.

To find the circumference around an uncharted world

he felt a tuning inside himself, the way

— for one hour each year —

a well holds a pillar of tropical sun.

The Standard

As small as a swallow

                    the soul on wing,

weighed by an ibis against a feather,

fed with a bowl of figs.

                    "I was loved

in this life,"

           the inscription reads,

with birds, snakes, and bundled sheaves,

meaning: "I am even loved now."

Dragonflies

mated in mid air. Hovering,

over the pond's leafy
platters,
   they could not know

that we were children and that
   this was the garden

      of the Tang empress,
who died
   believing her holy soul

would drop into nothingness
of nirvana,
   never to be reborn — her

hundreds of mirror-attendants
      with her, while
ten times as many did not know

they would die
    ten years on,
   only lithe characters
to face hollow eyes
      of machine
guns
   and Tiananmen cannon.

They could not know
    that Earth revolves.
The dead do return.

             We were poets,

after all, the way we dragged

       our sleeves

          through moon-

white water

         to see its bottom,

and soldiers,

       swashing bamboo sabers,

and scholars,

       inspecting iridescence

          on the wing.

The Great Wall of 1980

As kids, we were forbidden
from crossing streams
                among strangers.

The skulls of soldiers
                and peasants
were stacked too high
                for us to joke around.

The Great Wall had kept us free
from Mongol hordes,
                though on top of it

wind cut sharp
                as letter openers,
the shape of miniscule swords
that were sold
                in small, weary stalls
where buses stopped.

The incline was impossible
                to climb
listening to mothers ask,
        "What shoes should we have worn?"

The barbarian numbers
                were like grass,
and men who fell in the heat
                were buried inside the stone.

We believed
        in the emperors' famous cruelty

and so we asked
                     why so many soldiers
were walking around
                     without their guns.

And our guide said perfunctorily,
"Everyone must serve the state
                     and every
soldier should have vacation
                     like you."

The Harper

Cycladic,
        next to
the golden sauceboats
                and oons.
The head
           featureless as floor
like a Brancusi bird

disdains any hint it sees,
not wanting eyes, not
        even needing lines
for catgut
      or marble

to play by heart.

Stephen Bar Sudhaili

1.
"What exists when demon is no longer demon?"
      the mystic asked.

What if the answer were nothing?

2.
Beyond perception

      nothing stands between things,
         nothing bears distinction.

At time's end, no one perishes,
no thing

      is corrupted, nothing is missing.

All returns,
      sanctified, united,
      and confused
     (which translators also render "mingled"),

"God will be all, everything."
      Above all, through all, in all.

          "Who would call to whom,"
          Stephen asked, "if God is all?

And, who could answer, who speak, if all were one?"

The year was 500.

3.

So much flumoxed Philoxenus, he said something like: "We are not
dogs, nor is our God."

"Devils will not not burn.
                          The same for sinners.

Damnation is forever. And so is division.
For such is bliss."

"And . . . and . . . and . . .
                          his style is poor."

But oblivion's style was oblivion.

What is thought when all words stop?

4.

On the wall of his cell, Stephen did not even write his name, but left
just sympathy:

                 "all is all the same" by which he meant:
nothing

         will cleave maker from what is made,

nothing separate

                 the answer from its question,

                          or force bliss from all
         blisses.

In the Time of the Tang

Dragons were all-knowing
and were carved out of jade.

Monks caught fish and then
released them with one's sins.

Others swung switchblades
on strings, like helicopter blades.

Mistresses watched the peasants
from the windows of their cars

and laughed that they were made
of mud, or brick, or paper.

But, Heaven never blessed the mistresses.
No matter how often they beat bronze

or whitened their faces or
wrapped themselves in red.

They used to love their fingers and spent
their days growing nails as long as dragon

teeth, but hated toes and pinched them
until rosebuds were all their legs could sprout.

The country girls, by contrast, loved to walk
and spent long hours hunting birds

they couldn't kill. They liked to point out distant nests
then hide their fingers up their sleeves.

The Buddha's Smile

was never so broad or so jade

as when we stopped to take off our sneakers
and gently pile them among dime-thin sandals
and slippers of a thousand thousand pilgrims.

We had been warned that he could not
be purchased for all our happy money.

What could we offer him?

He had been gold before, after all,
and bronze and copper,
and stone ten thousand times.

To Ohio

I test transcendence.
Unless it is to spit grape seeds
or query the driver "How far?"
I hold my hand in my hand
and comb my mind for patience,
feigning death. One day
I could wake up in Ohio,
the straggler with greasy
French fries for hair, or
the mother asleep beneath
dancing Shiva, or the fraternity
brother, spoiled with brandy,
or the chatty octogenarian,
friendless, even among other
octogenarians: "I was born
before the car — you can't imagine
a world without asphalt ribbons, can you? —
I chose my destination with a dart
while my wife watched television.
I've done everything, I was
even a boxer and I invented a language:
You talk with knuckles; you can say
things you would never think."

Swan

An elegant arm fills its sleeve,
right down to its last black button.
What is it like to swim, head in open
air, with poise
                suspended
         in the substance that sustains you?

We too dream to live with all we need
in thought,
               to breathe in
empty air and with a word
                            fill
the long, dark throat of feeling.

The Lepton Event

"A neutrino passes through electrons
to emerge a neutrino"

                              the same as before.
Only barely having mass,

"its properties not yet fully grasped."

Transcend the smallest forms.

Can we ever really not exist?

Glimpsed from the outside, one imagines
a windshield that has suffered buckshot,
blue-white halos staring holes through glass
— eyes of ghosts or galaxies.

From the inside, like the idea of a wasp:
parabolic,

                    exploding in wings,
sailing straight through the fastness
of windows and despair.

Where Do I Begin

to finish in half
an hour, to settle words
like a talkative flock
of black birds on a line,
to quiet their caws
to just one voice, or none
at all — fold their black
into iridescent clean,
a beak pecking on top of scrawny
legs, one wide pupil swallowing all
the bright orange
                              fallen
to earth unnoticed, from
a too plump grocery sack?

An Index of What We Didn't Ask

How does the skin cover the bones, exactly?

What are the rules for applying the possessive 's?

In what contexts should "she" not stand for "us"?

Where do you put your ears when you sleep?

How small can you become without hurting those you love?

Of what does fire really consist?

How do things not wish to burn?

Where else do words exist?

August 6, 2011

We have been killing

words all day

in order to make dead

tongues speak

the ghost-light

force hiding

in Hama's aitch

Acknowledgments

Thanks and acknowledgments are given to the following journals in which some of the poems of this book first appeared:

"Aerialists" and "In the Time of the Tang," *Portland Review*

"The Buddha's Smile," *Cortland Review*

"Filled Like a Brush," *Potomac Review*

"The Lepton Event" and "Where Do I Begin," *Denver Quarterly*

"To Ohio," *Cimarron Review*

Some poems incorporate quotations from Francis Bacon, Jane Austen, JFK, and others.

PHOTO BY ROBIN REYMOND

ERIC REYMOND was raised in Topeka, Kansas and now lives outside New Haven, Connecticut. He is Senior Lector in Biblical Hebrew at Yale Divinity School. His research concerns ancient Hebrew and Aramaic, especially as this occurs in ancient poetry. His most recent book, *Qumran Hebrew*, explores the peculiarities of the Hebrew of the Dead Sea Scrolls.

ERIC REYMOND

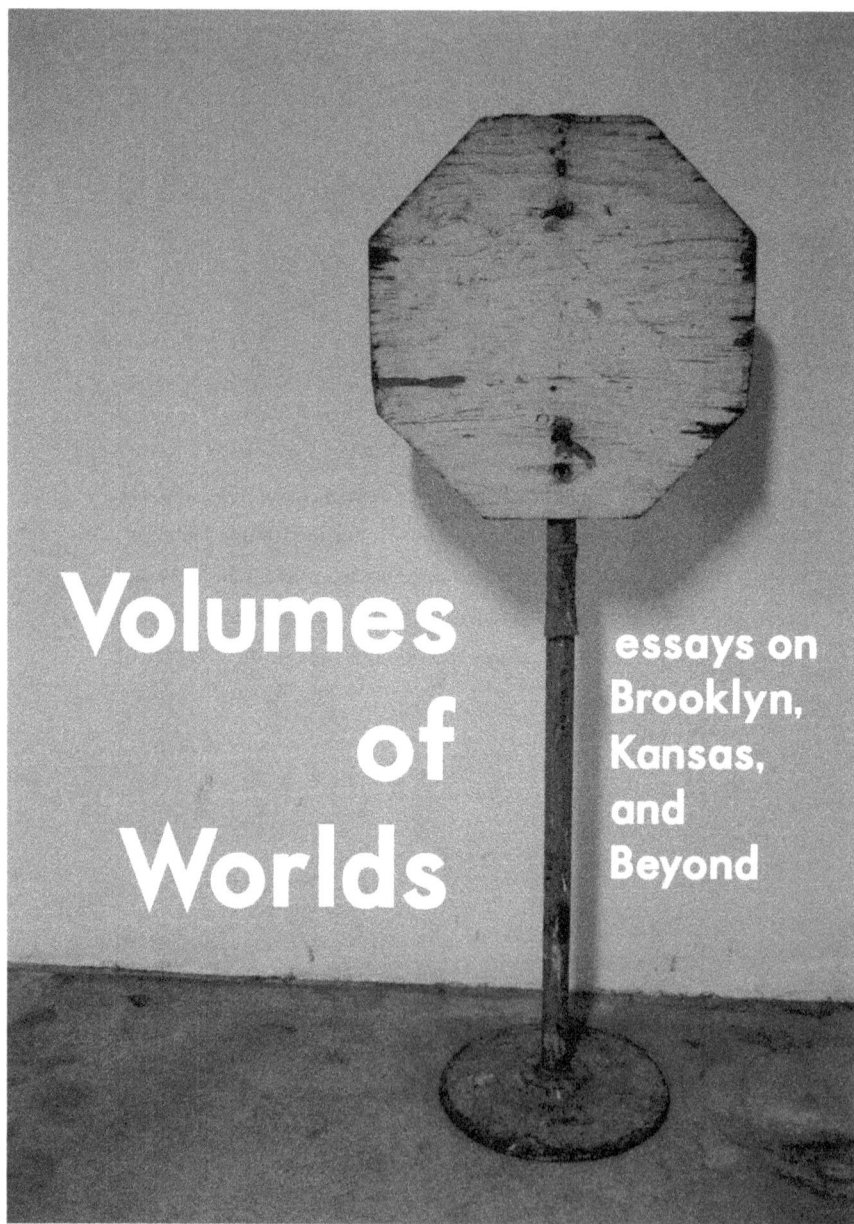

Volumes of Worlds

essays on Brooklyn, Kansas, and Beyond

SOFTCOVER, EBOOK, AND DELUXE HARDCOVER

#new texture

Eric Reymond
Sub-Sub Librarian, Extracts on a

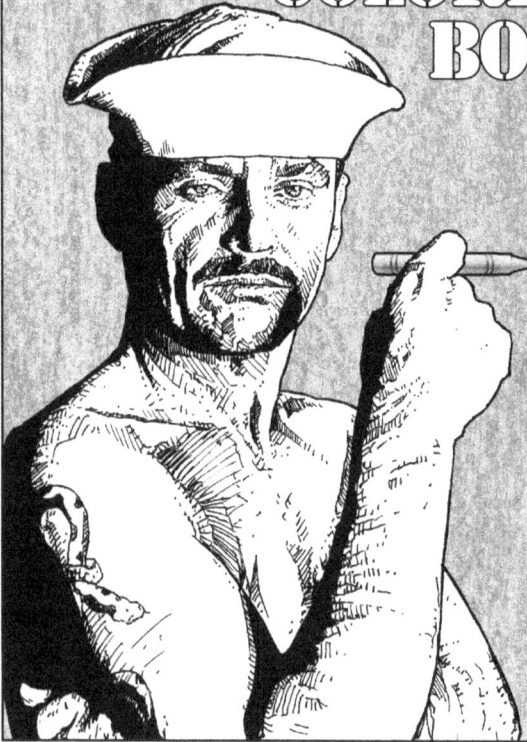

THE LAST COLORING BOOK

JIMMY ANGELINA and WYATT DOYLE

Ceci n'est pas un coloring book

lastcoloringbook.com

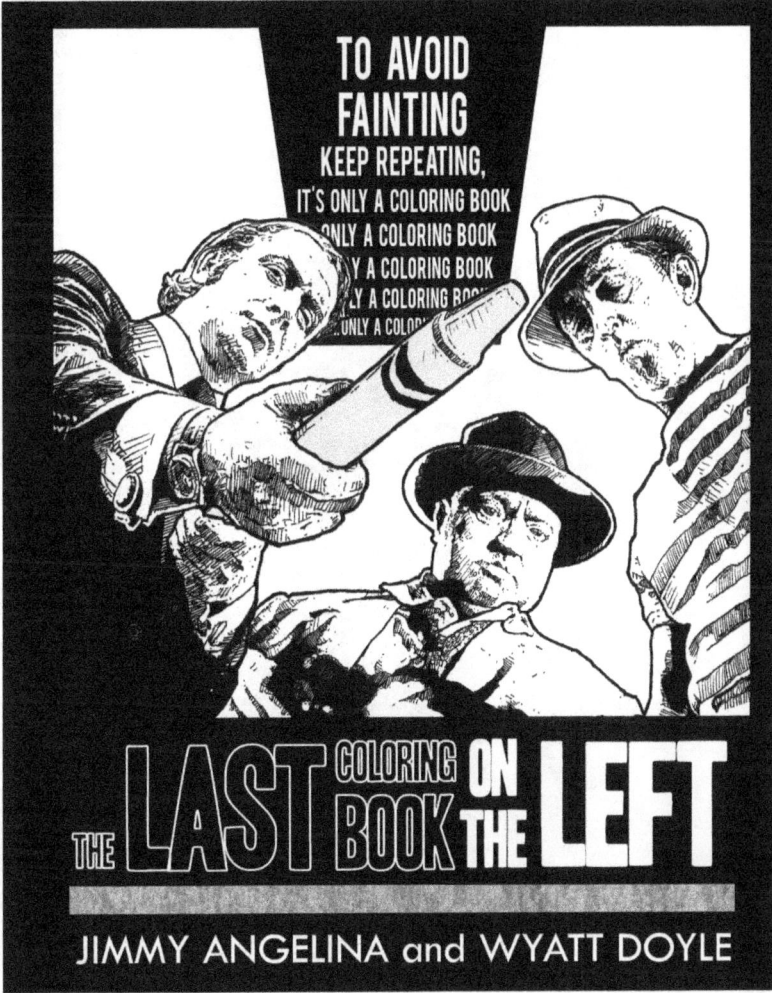

Ceci n'est pas un coloring book¹ non plus

new texture

WYATT DOYLE

STOP REQUESTED

WYATT DOYLE

ILLUSTRATIONS BY
STANLEY J. ZAPPA

WYATT DOYLE
DOLLAR HALLOWEEN

I need real tuxedos and a top hat!

words and pictures by wyatt doyle

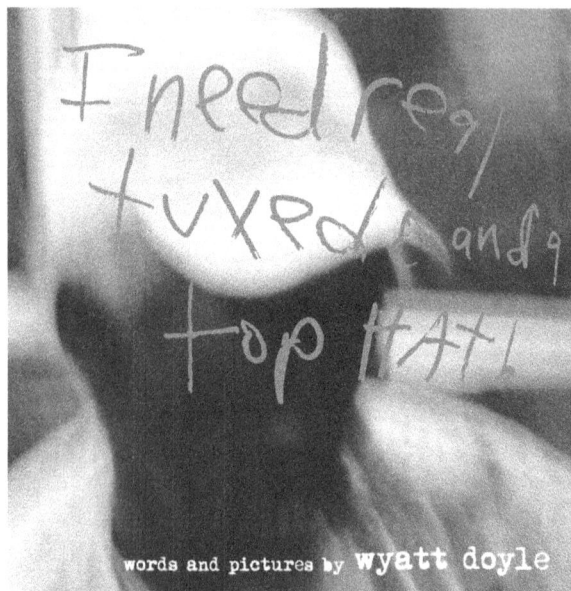

"[**Doyle**] has the elliptical, post-modern zen understatement of a Richard Brautigan, with a poet's gift for the carefully-chosen detail and a playwright's gift for dialogue.

"I admire his eye for the unexpected juxtapositions of detail among the seemingly mundane, juxtapositions of detail that provide a window of insight into life, into society, into truth. This quality is as strong in his fiction as it is in his photography."

—**Bill Shute**,
Kendra Steiner Editions

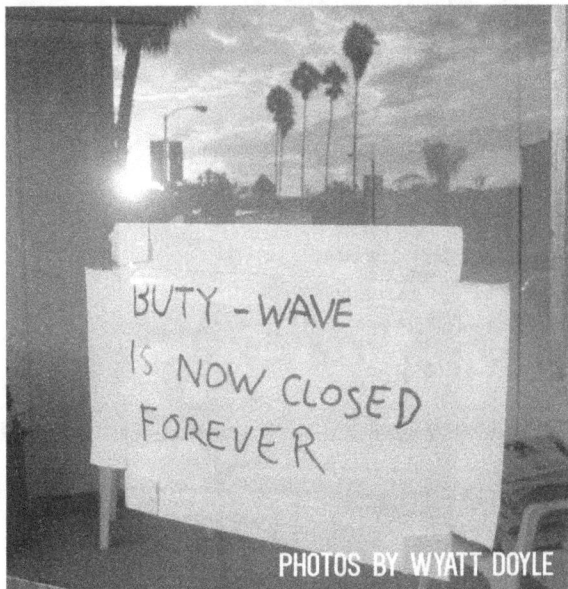

PHOTOS BY WYATT DOYLE

STOP REQUESTED *stories*
illustrated by Stanley J. Zappa
softcover and deluxe hardcover

DOLLAR HALLOWEEN *photographs*
hardcover

I NEED REAL TUXEDO AND A TOP HAT!
photographs/stories
88-pg softcover
104-pg deluxe hardcover

Jorge AMAYA doesn't Live Here ANYMORE

PHOTOS BY WYATT DOYLE

BUTY-WAVE IS NOW CLOSED FOREVER
photographs
88-pg softcover
104-pg deluxe hardcover

JORGE AMAYA DOESN'T LIVE HERE ANYMORE *photographs*
88-pg softcover
104-pg deluxe hardcover

new texture

Art: Samson Pollen

Books worth fighting over.

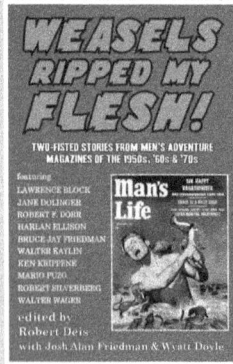

The Library is open.

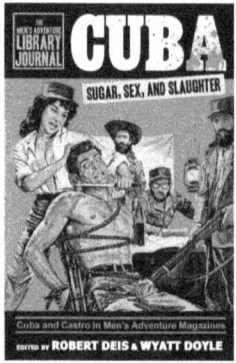

The Revolution will be on the Moon.

n u l u n a

Andrew Biscontini

new texture

www.ingramcontent.com/pod-product-compliance
Lightning Source LLC
Chambersburg PA
CBHW020604030426
42337CB00013B/1202